Real Wisdom:
How to Start and Sustain a Successful
Career in Real Estate

REBECCA DEL POZO

No part of this Book may be reproduced or transmitted in any form or by any means, electronic or mechanical, including photocopying, recording or by any information storage and retrieval system, without written permission from the author.

This book is presented solely for educational and entertainment purposes. The author and publisher are not offering it as legal, business, or other professional services advice. While best efforts have been used in preparing this book, the author and publisher make no representations or warranties of any kind and assume no liabilities of any kind with respect to the accuracy or completeness of the contents and specifically disclaim any implied warranties of merchantability or fitness of use for a particular purpose. Neither the author nor the publisher shall be held liable or responsible to any person or entity with respect to any loss or incidental or consequential damages caused, or alleged to have been caused, directly or indirectly, by the information contained herein.

The methods described within this Book are the author's personal thoughts. They are not intended to be a definitive set of instructions for obtaining a real estate license or operating a real estate business. You may discover there are other methods and materials that accomplish the same result.

Each Keller Williams office is individually owned and operated. Every brokerage and individual real estate office is different and the advice and strategies contained herein may not be suitable for your situation. You should seek the services of a competent professional before beginning any real estate education or certification program or joining a brokerage.

Copyright © 2018 Rebecca Del Pozo
All rights reserved.
ISBN: 1719441332
ISBN-13: 978-1719441339

Thank you, Mom & Dad, for always believing in me and supporting my big crazy dreams. To Tiff- thank you for reminding me how strong I am. Thank you Mike for always having my back. To Antonio, Tricia & Bella- I pray you always ask WHY NOT ME and go after your dreams. Special thank you to Gary Keller for creating this massive universe of opportunity, Althea Osborn for inspiring me, Mike Bastian for training me up, Dianna Kokoszka & my MAPS Mastery Coaches for teaching me to be BOLD, KWRI for the incredible tech & tools, Calvin Mergen for CTE, Jeff Albrecht & Colleen Dutmers for creating opportunity for me.

-Rebecca

TABLE OF CONTENTS

SECTION 1

INTRODUCTION	
DECIDING ON REAL ESTATE	9
REAL ESTATE CAREER MYTHS	
WAYS TO STRUCTURE A REAL ESTATE CAREER	
INTROVERTS AND REAL ESTATE	
STUDYING FOR, & PASSING YOUR EXAM	
CREATING A STUDY PLAN	29
TEN TIPS FOR EFFECTIVE STUDY TIME	34
STUDY OPTIONS: LIVE OR ONLINE CLASSES	40
HOW TO STUDY AND HAVE A LIFE	45
WHEN YOU HAVE A BAD DAY	50
TIPS FOR PASSING THE EXAM	54

SECTION 2

INTRODUCTION	
TIPS FOR PICKING A BROKERAGE	
WHO ARE YOU?	
REBECCA MATH	
WHAT EVERY NEW AGENT SHOULD KNOW	
SUCCESS AT SELF-EMPLOYMENT	81
THE PART-TIME REAL ESTATE AGENT	86
GOAL-SETTING	91
THE VALUE OF A COACH	97
RETIRING OUT OF REAL ESTATE	

SECTION 3

CONCLUSION
ABOUT THE AUTHOR

INTRODUCTION

I have big dreams! I believe I was created for greatness and so are you. We sometimes limit ourselves and don't think BIG enough.

One of my dreams is to have a worldwide network of friends. From day one of this journey in real estate, I felt the Lord say this was going to be marketplace ministry. I don't have it all figured out and trust me, I have failed forward on many, many, many occasions. But, I can tell you that this business has changed my life for the better and I believe it has the power to do the same for you.

I wrote this book for anyone who is considering a career in real estate. It's the book I wish I'd had when I was an *aspiring* agent. It's also the book I wish I'd had as a *new* agent. It's a collection of advice and of lessons learned (some the easy way and others the hard way) over the course of my many years in the business.

So, wherever you are in your journey, I truly believe there's something—hopefully many somethings—that will help you navigate these waters more easily and successfully.

When I started in real estate, I had no college degree, no business experience, and a very small network of local contacts. My success isn't magic. It's the result of joining a great brokerage; one that provided me with tons of coaching and education; and following the map to success that they shared with me, to the letter. And you can too. You can build the business and the career you want, whatever your age, education or background.

This book is the first step.

Here's my fine print disclaimer: I'm a Keller Williams (KW) agent through and through. I'm so thankful Gary Keller has created such a large universe that we can have our own individual worlds within it.

You may read this and think to yourself "gosh, she's talking about KW a lot, and it's true. This is the only life I've ever known in real estate. I've been fully immersed in KW, so much of what I share is with the intention to influence you to join a KW office and say it's because Rebecca told me to!

Deciding on Real Estate

Are you looking for a career change? Have you always been interested in real estate, but not known what it would take to get your license and build a career? Or has real estate caught your attention only recently, and now you're wondering whether you've got what it takes to be a success?

If a real estate career is on your radar at all, then this section is for you. In it, I explore the myths and truths about what this career is and is not. I orient you to the possibilities it offers and I address some of the self-imposed limitations that often stop people from pursuing this career before they've really started.

Real Estate Career Myths

What follows are a few of the myths or misconceptions I hear from people about real estate careers. It's by no means a comprehensive list, but these are the ones I find myself responding to most often.

Misconception #1: It's easy.
It's not. It is a very rewarding career. It's a career that's challenging in some wonderful ways. It's a career in which you have the potential to define and achieve success. But it isn't easy.

We work hard to earn a license and to stay current on the laws that regulate our industry. We spend time building our reputations and relationships, so that we can have long-lasting careers.

I tell the aspiring agents I work with that I use the word "career" and don't use the word "job," deliberately. Because at Keller Williams, agents are essentially building businesses within the larger company. We set our own goals and make plans for reaching them. As our businesses grow, we can hire our own support staff, transaction coordinators, marketing specialists, showing assistants and listing agents.

Misconception #2: Agents will do *anything* for a sale.
My experience hasn't been the "cut throat" sales experience that many claim to have in this field. I appreciate that KW requires us all to be Realtors. This means we are the true professionals in the real estate world. We don't view our colleagues as competition, we are business partners. The agents I work with and have gotten to know over the years are some of the most supportive and encouraging people I've ever met. They are incredibly generous with their time and knowledge.

Keller Williams really fosters this culture with our new agent coaching program. There are many examples in my own market center of agents going out of their way to help their colleagues—new agents, especially. Here's just one example. I work with an agent who has the corner on a particularly large market in our area. When new agents join our market center he'll let them work his (many) open houses. This gives them the chance to meet prospective clients and gain valuable experience.

Secondly, the National Association of Realtors (NAR) has a code of ethics and standards of practice that all their members commit to honoring. There are laws that govern what Realtors can and cannot do and say. At Keller Williams we formalized our own belief system and gave it a name, **WI4C2TS©**. It guides how we treat each other and our clients. Here it is and what it means:

WIN-WIN or no deal.
INTEGRITY do the right thing
CUSTOMERS always come first
COMMITMENT in all things
COMMUNICATION seek first to understand
CREATIVITY ideas before results
TEAMWORK together everyone achieves more
TRUST starts with honesty
SUCCESS results through people

Misconception #3: It's expensive to get started.

It does cost money for licensing, that's true. But it's a far, far smaller financial investment than say, a four-year college degree. The cost varies by state, so I can't give you a number that will be accurate for you. Don't assume it's financially out of reach though. You can easily research the costs in your area. If there's a brokerage you think you might want to work for once you're licensed, they can help you figure out what you need to budget for study materials, licensing exams and other fees.

Misconception #4: If I'm not a natural salesperson, I won't be successful.

I would say that you must be a good communicator and a good teacher, but not necessarily a "sales person," by the traditional definition. You need the ability to talk to people; to connect with them; to hear what their needs are and gauge whether your skills and approach are a good fit for them. And then you need the ability to communicate who you are and what you offer in a genuine way. Lots of successful agents don't have a "sales" background.

Misconception #5: Real estate careers are a good side gig/part-time job.
It's impossible to stay current on all the laws, regulations and details required to represent clients well if you aren't in it full-time. There are just too many moving pieces and the consequences of missing something are too grave to "part-time" this career. I would recommend doing everything in your power to make the transition from part-time to full-time as quickly as possible, so that you are providing the best care you possibly can to your clients at all times.

If you find yourself in a position where you must balance two careers at one time, you would benefit from joining a team, so that you can have the support you need and your clients receive the best care possible. Or you could just operate as a referral business, where you refer clients to other agents and collect a percentage of that agent's commission when the transaction closes.

This is a great option for people who can't be 100% dedicated to the business. I'll talk more about options for part-time real estate careers later in this book.

Exploring the Possibilities: Ways to Structure a Real Estate Career

People often think of being a real estate agent as only representing clients in the purchase or sale of a property. That's how I started my career and may be how you start yours too. But it doesn't have to be the only way you put your skills to work.

I'm a big fan of variety and of diversifying sources of income, including building in passive income opportunities where I can. I want to share with you some of the ways you can do that as a real estate agent. Keep in mind that my experience has been with Keller Williams exclusively, so the opportunities I discuss in this chapter are the ones available with KW. I don't know for sure what other brokerages offer.

Option 1: Representing buyers and sellers. As a real estate agent, clients will hire you to represent them in the purchase or sale of a property.

Option 2: "Flipping" properties. This is where you buy a property, invest in renovating it, and then sell it for a profit. As a licensed real estate agent, you can represent yourself as buyer and seller and you'll have access to new properties as they come on the market.

Option 3: Investment properties. This is where you purchase a property and then rent it out to a third party. Again, Keller Williams has educational materials to help agents do this successfully, maximize their earning potential, and avoid some of the mistakes people commonly make when starting out as landlords.

Option 4: Referrals. I know agents whose entire business is built on Keller Williams' Referral Program. Keller Williams has agents licensed to sell homes almost anywhere in the world. If someone approaches you wanting to purchase or sell a home outside of the area in which you work, you can refer them to a Keller Williams agent in that region. If that client hires that Keller Williams agent and they purchase or sell a property, you receive a portion of the commission on that sale, just for referring that client. Pretty great, right?

Option 5: Profit-Sharing. This one is a unique option within the world of real estate. When you close a transaction, you pay a percentage of your commission to Keller Williams, until you've paid the company dollar CAP in commission for a calendar year. After that commitment is met, then you keep 100% of the commissions you make for the remainder of that calendar year.

Here's where profit-sharing comes in. The person who "referred" you to Keller Williams gets a thank-you from KW owners in the form of profit-share check. When you go into business with Keller Williams, you're a stakeholder on DAY 1. When you recommend a friend or acquaintance and they join as an agent (anywhere in the world) and name you as their sponsor, you could take part in profit-share. The benefit can outlive you and be passed along to your heirs. If you want up to date details on vesting requirements, please reach out to me. My contact information is included at the end of the book.

Option 6: Salaried positions. For whatever reason, maybe you want a more predictable 9-5, salaried career. Keller Williams hires licensed real estate agents to provide administrative and transaction support. So, you could use your knowledge and skills in this way as opposed to directly representing buyers and sellers.

If you want to dive more deeply into any of these possibilities, here are a few of my favorite books on the subject: *The Millionaire Real Estate Agent; The Millionaire Real Estate Investor; Flip: How to Find, Fix and Sell Houses for Profit; Hold: How to Find Buy and Rent Houses for Wealth;* and *The One Thing: The Surprisingly Simple Truth Behind Extraordinary Results.*

I'm an Introvert. Can I Be a Great Realtor?

Being an introvert is not the same as being shy, although you *can* be both. It doesn't mean you don't like people or lack social skills.

The truth is that there are wonderful things about being an introvert and there are successful and influential people who reportedly identify as such: Bill Gates, Albert Einstein, Meryl Streep, JK Rowling, Warren Buffett and Dr. Seuss, just to name a few.

Whether you're an introvert or an extrovert really speaks to which kinds of activities energize you and which kinds drain you.

Introverts find social situations draining, and are energized by quiet, solitary and creative pursuits. That doesn't mean they can't be social and charming (they totally can!). It just means that they'd prefer not to and when they are required to be, they must plan for downtime afterward to recover.

All of that brings me back to the question posed by the title of this chapter--is being an introvert at odds with being a great Realtor?

I think to answer that accurately, we must bust the myth that as Realtors we are primarily in the sales business. While it's true that we are helping people with the biggest purchase they will ever make, at its core, this business isn't about selling; it's about building relationships. Something, incidentally, that introverts are good at.

Introverts tend to be good listeners and spend more time doing that than they do speaking. In a real estate context, where so much of your success depends upon listening and understanding what a client wants, that tendency can come in very handy.

So, the short answer to the question posed by the title of this chapter is, yes, I do think introverts can be great Realtors. And extroverts can too!

I just think the strengths that extroverts have are much more celebrated and are commonly seen as more desirable than those of introverts. In an industry like real estate, it's especially important to highlight that introverts' strengths are different but can be just as advantageous.

For more information about some of the strengths associated with being an introvert, check out Susan Cain's book, *Quiet: The Power of Introverts in a World that Can't Stop Talking*.

Another book I love that has a business application is Beth Buelow's, *The Introvert Entrepreneur*.

Studying for & Passing Your Real Estate License Exam

Before you can get to the fun part, you've got to get through the not-so-fun part: completing the requisite clock hours (studying) and passing your state and national licensing exams.

There's a lot to learn and much of the content is dense. But, there are some ways you can structure your study and exam preparation time to maximize your efficiency and increase your chances of passing your exam on the first try.

What follows in this section is some practical advice. And I know it works because it is exactly what an agent on my team did last year when she was navigating this process.

Creating a Study Plan

You've signed-up for your clock hours. Maybe you've even logged in and looked at your online courses—or better yet, started them.

And then something happens that pushes you headfirst into the reality of the studying experience. For one aspiring agent I worked with it was the arrival of the box of heavy textbooks on her doorstep. That was when the scope of the task at hand became apparent to her.

You may start to worry about the sheer volume of information you have to learn and wonder about how to tackle all of it effectively. What follows are some recommendations for approaching the studying experience.

Set *realistic*, time-bound goals. Take the total study time required in hours and then look at your schedule. Figure out how many hours per week you can realistically devote to studying. If you have a full-time job, it's probably less than if you are working part-time or not working at all. If you have children or other family commitments, that probably decreases your study time too. Identify the actual hours on the actual days you'll be studying. Picking 20-hours a week as a goal is useless if there's no way you can realistically complete that many hours.

Whatever the number of hours you commit to, add those study sessions to your calendar on specific days. Make it an appointment and don't schedule anything else during those periods.

Set an exam date. You probably won't actually be able to schedule your exam until you finish the required clock hours. But, you can count out how many weeks you think it will take to work through the material, given the weekly goals you set for yourself, and then pick a week when you plan to take the exam. Write it on your calendar and tell your accountability coach (discussed later in this chapter) what it is.

Track your study time. I'd recommend creating a time-sheet to track the time you spend studying. Excel works well for this.

Create external accountability. Find someone who will serve as a check on your adherence to your study plan. Pick a day of the week when you'll email or call to say whether you met your study goal for the week.

It's easy to skip a study session when there's no one who will know if you do. If you pick a brokerage before you start studying, your contact there might be a good accountability partner. But you could also ask a friend, a partner, your mom, or a sibling—anyone you think will hold your feet to the fire.

Pick the right study method. The online method is great if you want to go at your own pace and study from home. But, if you thrive in a classroom setting, or if you know you'll get distracted by other things if you study from home, then you might want to pursue a live class option. There is no right or wrong--it's just about being honest about what works best for you. Picking a method because it's what you wish worked best is a recipe for frustration.

Leave time for review…but not too much. Build in some time (maybe a week or so) for general review, and for concentrated review of those sections that challenge you. But be careful not to over-study. You could theoretically study forever, but it's not a good idea. Follow your study and review plans, take as many practice exams as you can and then book the real thing. Just get it over with. The worst thing that can happen is you fail, in which case you'll just take it again. And this time, you'll know what to expect.

Ten Tips for Efficient and Effective Study Time

Skip the study guide. Some of the licensing course providers include a cram section with their online courses. It's part of the test prep and sample exam feature and it walks you through the crucial concepts. It's, essentially, an electronic study guide at your fingertips. So, no need to make one of your own. I highly recommend selecting an education provider that includes these features.

Teach it to someone else. Explaining concepts or terms to someone else, helps cement those things in your memory. Find a friend, colleague or relative who's willing to listen. It makes a big difference.

Take breaks. Limit the number of hours you devote to studying at one sitting. Getting up every hour and walking around, grabbing a snack or chatting with a friend for five to ten-minutes is a good idea.

If you don't take breaks, you'll stop paying attention. Your mind will wander. You'll be tempted to go online and read the news or check your email. You won't retain much of anything. And your eyes will get really tired.

Get some context. Working part-time in a real estate office is a great way to get some real-world experience and context for what you're studying.

If you don't or can't work for a real estate agent, maybe there are ways you can get a similar experience. Chances are someone you know knows an agent. Maybe you could invite them for coffee and conduct an informational interview. Ask them about some of the things you're most interested in or challenged by, with respect to your studies.

Do an inventory of your skills. Are you a great writer? If so, maybe a local agent would love some help with content for their website, or writing a blog, or managing their social media accounts. Offer your help for free a couple of hours per week in exchange for getting some experience in the industry. There are legal limitations in terms of the kinds of activities you're allowed to do without a real estate license though, so make sure whatever you propose or whatever they suggest, complies with applicable laws.

Pay attention to your study space. Give yourself the gift of a comfortable space that's conducive to studying. Make sure you have enough light to see properly. Get yourself a comfortable chair and a desk with enough space for your computer, notebook and whatever else you need close at hand. If you need it quiet, set-up in a room with a door, away from the activity of the house. If your house is always noisy, find somewhere quiet, such as a college library, to do your studying.

Have some water nearby, turn your phone off (or switch it to silent). Make sure your space is supporting your goals and is a place you won't avoid because it's not functional or it's physically uncomfortable.

Conduct periodic reviews. Don't wait until you've finished working through all the material before reviewing it. After completing two or three lessons, look through those slides again and make sure you can pass the lesson quizzes. It reinforces the material and won't take much extra time.

Take ALL of the pop quizzes you can. Pretty self-explanatory, right?

Get outside. I used to do this when I worked full-time in an office and noticed fatigue and/or lack of focus setting in. Go outside for five-minutes and stand on your deck or walk around the neighborhood.

Breathe in fresh air. Get your eyes away from the computer screen. It makes all the difference when you come back. You need a variety of sensory stimulation for your brain to work properly and for you to feel your best. So much of what we do now is on computers, phones, tablets or Kindles. We must make an effort to step away and spend some time in the kinds of environments our bodies were made to enjoy.

Prioritize sleep. This is good advice for all of life but is especially true when you're trying to learn something new and/or when you're preparing for a big test. There is also some evidence that if you study for a few minutes before you go to sleep, your brain will retain that information better than if you'd studied it that morning.

If you are going to try that, I'd recommend studying from your textbook or other notes rather than online. Screen time before bed is associated with difficulty falling asleep and more restless sleep.

Take the sample exams. If you're going to fail or get something wrong, you'd rather do that on a practice exam than on the real deal. The practice exams often have the questions you'll see on the real exam, or very similar ones.

Online Studying or Live Classes? What's the Best Approach?

You have the option of completing your clock hours either online or in a live class format. Both are legitimate. Both have impressive exam pass rates to recommend them. So, how do you know which one is right for you? Here are a few indicators that online is the way to go.

You rock at time management and organization. You know how to design an effective study schedule and you know you will stick to it without outside supervision/structure. You can break down a large amount of content into manageable pieces, without getting overwhelmed by the whole. You are confident that you can accurately estimate how long each piece will take and then extrapolate that to determine a realistic target exam date.

You're independent. You will show up for your studying shifts even if no one else knows you did. You know how to dig deeper on concepts or terms that you don't understand and how to find the information you need online or in your textbooks. But you also know when you need to ask for help from an expert, how to do that, and aren't afraid to do so.

You want to go at your own pace. Which, by the way, could be more quickly or more slowly than an in-person class is likely to go. You don't want to be rushed through lessons that challenge you and you don't want to be held back on sections that you find easy or straightforward. It would frustrate you equally to sit in a class and listen to concepts you already understand explained multiple times; or to feel like the only person in the room who was struggling with a concept.

You have an accountability partner already. You have someone who has agreed to check-in with you regularly. Someone who knows the study goals (hours and exam date) you've set for yourself. Someone to whom you will have to confess if you don't reach them. Someone who will call you on it if your target exam date comes and goes and you're still re-reading lesson five from the Fundamentals course.

You need flexibility. Whether it's because of your work schedule, family or other obligations, you can't commit to being in a classroom on the same night every week for an extended period.

You're comfortable with technology. You're comfortable with computers and navigating online course formats. You know how to pace yourself so that you give your eyes a break from the screen. The idea of sitting in front of a computer for 90-hours over the course of a couple of months studying this stuff doesn't make you shudder.

You don't need face-to-face time. It doesn't help you to discuss concepts with classmates, and/or you have people in your life who are happy to listen to you talk about what you're learning so that you can cement the concepts in your brain. You are okay with hours of independent work and you don't crave a sense of camaraderie in this process.

There aren't any live courses available/the timeframe of live courses isn't convenient. If there are no live classes in your area, you'll be forced to study online. We host one in our office, so I'd encourage you to reach out to your local Keller Williams market center if you're interested in the live option and ask them if they offer that in their office.

I want to close by saying that none of the qualities I've listed above are objectively better or worse than their opposites. They're just different. Different people work best in different environments, but it's not a value judgement. The idea really is to be honest with yourself about yourself and then pick strategies that will set you up for success.

How to Study and…Have a Life

The older I get the more difficult it seems to take on new adventures. Not because I don't want to. Not because I'm lazier than I was before. Not because I'm not as smart or dedicated as I used to be. Not because my work ethic has changed. It's just that the older we get the more things we're trying to manage—job, family, kids, social or philanthropic commitments—you get the idea.

I don't claim to have the answers. But, I can share some ideas. And maybe one of those ideas will help you. Or maybe it will spark another idea that will be the difference between whether this whole thing seems like a pipe dream or whether it starts to look so achievable that you can see your name on that real estate license.

Be realistic about how much time you can devote to studying. This is dense stuff. And if you're going into it with little or no knowledge of the ins and outs of the real estate business, it's going to be a lot of information to cram into your brain. Maybe it will take months instead of weeks for you to get through the material. Better to spend one or two hours on it a day, than to try to cram in two or three times that in order to finish in a few weeks.

Having a target date to work toward helps you stay accountable, but it also reminds you that this won't last forever!

Give something else up, temporarily. There are only so many hours in the day. If you've got a full schedule already, chances are something is going to have to give short-term, so you can find those hours to study. You could get up an hour early and spend that time with a cup of coffee and your study materials. Or maybe you sacrifice your lunch hour at work a couple of times a week.

No matter how many hours you do, be consistent. Working on it a little every day is way better than trying to hit your 10 hour/week goal all in one day.

Write down your study time goals on a calendar or in a journal and then cross off the hours as you complete them. I don't know about you, but I need visual representations of progress to stay motivated. Crossing off study sessions is really gratifying.

You can also set rewards for yourself. For example, meeting your study goal one week may mean you get to go to a movie, or buy new music for your iPod. Maybe you treat yourself to a spa day or a weekend getaway when you've passed your test.

Be sneaky with studying. Take some flash cards with key terms or concepts everywhere you go. Keep them in your coat pocket, your car, your purse, or the bag you take to work. When you find yourself with time on your hands--say sitting in the waiting room at the dentist's office, or waiting for a friend to show up for a coffee date--break out your cards and do a few minutes of studying. It all adds up!

Give yourself permission to say "no," and then do it. You will inevitably be invited to something or asked for help on a day and at a time that conflicts with studying. It's okay to say no. There are obvious exceptions--work requirements, family commitments, etc.--that aren't voluntary. But don't spread yourself too thin by agreeing to optional activities if you're already managing a jam-packed life and study schedule.

When You Have a Bad Day

(What follows below is an excerpt from a blog post written by an agent on my team as she was studying for her real estate license exam. I thought it would be helpful for you to read it just in case you have a bad day or two on your studying journey.)

I sat down today to write a post I've had planned for a week now, but instead I'm writing this one. I'm writing this one because I am burned-out. And frustrated. And tired. And today, this whole thing feels impossible.

Or maybe not impossible, but close to it. Today I tried hard to study. Today I just couldn't. Today I am overwhelmed.

And maybe you are too. Or maybe you aren't today, but you were yesterday. Or will be tomorrow. Anyway, it seems dishonest or disingenuous to me to write a post with study tips when I'm struggling so much.

So, I'm not going to write that post. Instead I'm writing this one.

I'm writing, in part, because writing is how I express myself. It's how the jumble of thoughts and feelings get out of my brain and I release myself from the burden of carrying them around with me.

That's my first tip for recovering from a bad day. Whether you're a write-it-down kind of person, like me, or whether you're a talk it out person--do that thing. Vent your fears, or frustrations in whatever (healthy) way appeals to you.

But I'm also writing it down because that's how I figure out whether this is just a bad day, or whether it's the culmination of many days of doing too much with too little rest.

I chose to share it on the blog because there's nothing worse than struggling with something and thinking you're the only one. Or thinking that because it's a struggle, it's a sign you've made a huge mistake and never should have pursued whatever the thing is that's overwhelming you at the moment.
So, if you're having a rough day or a rough week: I'm with you.

This is hard. Becoming a real estate agent brings with it huge responsibilities, and it makes sense that studying to become one would be a huge responsibility too.

Social media, including blogs, often only show the parts of our lives we want other people to see. The pretty parts. The parts where it looks like we've got it all together. The parts where we make it all look easy. And effortless. But that's not life.

Sometimes life is pretty. And easy. And effortless. And sometimes we do have it all together. But sometimes we don't. I don't. That doesn't mean this was all a big mistake. Or that I'm failing.

If this is more than just a bad day for you too, it's okay to re-structure how you're studying. Give yourself some days off; decrease the number of study hours you've committed to; reward yourself with some fun or pampering; give yourself permission to sleep more; etc.

The Big Day: Tips for Passing Your Exam

You've finished your clock hours, now what?

It's time to make a plan for reviewing the content and preparing for the exam. Yay! Below is the path an agent on my team took for this process.

Take a baseline sample exam. Some education providers include a test prep section with the courses you purchase. I recommend selecting one that offers several practice exams and other tools to help you structure your study time.

It's a good idea to take a sample exam before you do any review to get a baseline of how close you are to being ready to take the test. The sample exam will show you the questions you got wrong, and many of them will break down the test by topic area and tell you the sections you most need to review.

Schedule your exam. You would think that having the exam on the calendar would up the stress factor, but weirdly it tends to decrease it. I think knowing that it's going to be over by a set date helps, emotionally. And having a date to work backward from gives structure to review time.

Review areas of weakness. After taking each sample exam, write down the sections you failed and review *only* them. Repeat this process after each sample exam.

Take every sample exam and quiz. Work back from the date of your exam and figure out how many you need to take each day to take them all by test day. This will help you get used to how questions on the exam are structured and help you see places where wording might bait you into picking the wrong answer.

Review every sample exam result. Look at the questions you get wrong first and make sure you understand why the correct answer is correct. Then review the whole exam, looking at the questions you get right too.

Sometimes you may be guessing, and you happened to pick the right one. Make sure you know why each correct answer is correct.

Account for memorization. The sample exams often repeat questions, as do the quizzes. They tell you not to rely on memorization, but it's hard not to when you've seen the same questions a couple of times. So, when you recognize a question and remember what the answer is, go through each of the other answers and tell yourself why it was the wrong one. When those terms or concepts then appear on the final exam in a different context, you'll know what they mean and can apply them in whatever context they appear.

Flash cards. If there are concepts you continue to have a hard time understanding or remembering, make some flash cards and review them for a few minutes several times throughout the day. Formulas and laws lend themselves well to flash card review.

You're a Licensed Agent! Now What?

Congratulations! You've studied hard and passed that exam. Now you're ready to start your business. First thing you should do is call me!! I mean it, reach out via FB or email at <u>rebeccad@kw.com</u>. I will celebrate with you! This is a HUGE accomplishment and it MUST be celebrated!

There are some important things to consider, as you put all those things you learned in theory, into practice.

This section addresses some of the big decisions you'll need to make, and the things you'll need to consider as you build a sustainable and successful career.

Tips for Picking a Brokerage

I've been with Keller Williams for my entire real estate career and I cannot imagine working anywhere else! For many reasons—the interdependent business model, the continuing education, support and coaching opportunities, and the technology resources (the list goes on!)—I truly believe it is the best brokerage, bar none.

But, there are other brokerages that might be a better fit, depending upon your personality, goals, working style or preferred business model.

No matter where you ultimately decide to put your talents to work, make sure you've asked the questions (and received the answers) you need to make an informed decision. To help you a bit with that, I'll share the five questions I'd encourage you to ask real estate brokerages before you decide which one is right for you.

What business model does their company employ? Is it an independent model in which you are completely on your own as an agent—essentially owning your own business with all the risks and rewards that can entail?

Is it a dependent model, in which you are an employee subject to their rules, regulations and job descriptions?

Or is it an interdependent model (Keller Williams fits into this model)? As you may have guessed, an interdependent model combines many of the best parts about independent and dependent models. In this model you get all the perks that come with a big-name brokerage: name recognition, access to technology and educational, coaching, staff and other resources. At the same time, you get to build your own business under the brokerage's umbrella. You get to set your own goals and build a business that is the size and scope you want.

What are their commission splits and office fees? Do you ever sell enough that you get to keep 100% of your commission? This is a very big deal. You need to know how much of what you bring in is going to go back to the brokerage and for what. And whatever that percentage is, you must decide whether you think it's a fair tradeoff for the support and resources you're getting from that company and how it compares to the other brokerages for whom you could work.

At Keller Williams you do get to keep 100% of your commission, once you've reached your annual responsibility to the company. As of this writing, once I've paid $19,000 to my local Keller Williams market center, I get to keep 100% of any other commissions I make. This amount varies by office, so I encourage you to reach out to me and I will refer you to someone at a Keller Williams in your area who can give you the number that will apply to you.

What kind of training is provided and what does that training cost you? You'll want to know what kinds of educational opportunities exist for you at whatever brokerage you select. And I mean formal, established programs. If you want to move into a leadership role, is there a curriculum you can follow to learn what you need to know to do that? If you want to start investing in properties and being a landlord as part of your business plan, does that brokerage have a program to help you be successful in that venture? Is there a mentoring or coaching program established at that brokerage, in which you could be matched with a more experienced agent who has a career similar to the one you want to pursue for yourself?

Ask to see a list of the educational and coaching programs that brokerage offers and make sure that the things that are of interest to you are available.

What kind of technical support is provided and what does that cost? By tech support, I don't mean someone who can fix your computer if it breaks, although that is worth knowing too! When I talk about technology in this context, I mean does the brokerage provide you with the following:

- A Website
- A Contact Management Database
- A Personal Mobile App
- Listing Syndication (and to how many sites?)
- Technology Training
- Marketing Materials

What kind of support/support staff is provided? Does the brokerage have administrative support to offer you? How about transaction coordinators to handle the paperwork and manage the due dates associated with the purchase or sale of a home? If so, how many hours per week will you have access to that support and how much will you pay for that? Will they provide you with a computer, a printer, copier or other practical support you need to do your job?

These questions are by no means a comprehensive list of things to ask, but they are a good place to start.

Who Are You?

As you think about starting and growing your career in real estate, it's important to think about what sets you apart from other agents.

Anyone with a real estate license can help someone purchase or sell a home, so what makes you different? Why would someone choose to work with you over the agent in the office across the hall or across town? What do you offer?

This isn't to say that you need to reinvent the wheel here—chances are there will be other agents with a value proposition that's similar to yours.

The purpose of this exercise is to get you to the point where you can, in 30-seconds or less, identify who you are as a real estate professional and the value that you bring to your clients.

I'll share mine with you, so you can see an example of what I mean.

At Rebecca Del Pozo & Company, we focus on three things:
- **We make our seller clients the most money possible, and we negotiate the best deal possible for our buyer clients.**
- **We do that in the least amount of time.**
- **And we do that with the least amount of hassle.**

You don't need to make it complicated for it to be good. In fact, I'd encourage you to keep it simple.

Make sure your value proposition is reflected in what you do and how you do it. But also make sure that you include it in your marketing and communication efforts too (videos, website, printed collateral, etc.).

Rebecca Math

Math was never my favorite subject in school, but the math I want to share with you here is a fun kind of math. It's an equation that goes something like this: **one real estate agent, with one real estate license equals four distinct businesses.** And that means four potential income streams!

Yep, in my world, 1+1 = 4. Let me tell you how.

The first is your real estate sales—how many families you serve in the purchase or sale of a home.

The second is investing in real estate yourself. Maybe you'll buy properties and then rent them out. Or maybe you'll purchase properties, renovate them and then sell them for a profit.

The third is referrals. Referrals in real estate have been a huge blessing in my life. Once you're licensed in one state as a real estate broker, you can literally refer a client to an agent anywhere in the world and receive a commission for doing so. You make the match between client and agent, and when that transaction closes you get a percentage of that agent's commission on the sale.

And finally, you'll have your profit-share business. This applies to Keller Williams specifically. It's not universal across other brokerages. Profit-share is about people and it's a simple concept: as you go about your business of serving clients, you will meet people who are agents with other brokerages, or who will tell you they're interested in transitioning to a career in real estate. And they'll ask you how you did it, how you like it, and what you think of Keller Williams.

As you inspire others to join Keller Williams, they will name you as the person most influential in their decision to join the company. Whenever that agent makes a sale in the future, Keller Williams will thank you with a check, representing a percentage of the company's profit from that sale.

Sometimes it's a check for $40, but there are people who make hundreds or thousands of dollars every month through profit-share. It just depends upon how many people you inspire to join and then how many transactions they close each month.

As I write this, there are people in the company who are on track to make over $1 million this year from profit-share alone. Wow.

Gary Keller, co-founder of Keller Williams, has written several books that serve as roadmaps to success in all four businesses, or business divisions, mentioned above. *The Millionaire Real Estate Agent; The Millionaire Real Estate Investor; Flip: How to Find, Fix and Sell Houses for Profit; Hold: How to Find Buy and Rent Houses for Wealth;* and *The One Thing: The Surprisingly Simple Truth Behind Extraordinary Results*, are just a few of my favorites.

What Every New Agent Should Know

The term "brand" is thrown around so much now, that it's become a buzzword and something that can be tempting to ignore. But you really do need to be able to communicate who you are and what sets you apart from other agents from the beginning. It's important. So, here are a few of my tips. Hope they help you!

Know your strengths. This is a slightly simpler version of knowing your value proposition. I had no idea how to do this when I was starting out. Keller Williams' *IGNITE* Program does this in the first class session, so if you join us you'll go through our process for answering the questions that will clarify this for you.

It's a basic series of questions, really. What are you known for? What are your strengths? How would someone describe you in three words? Ask a former employer, co-worker and an employee (if you ever supervised people) how they would describe you. This can be a great starting point.

Develop your network. When I started I didn't know *anyone*. My relatives were all in Canada and my only circle of acquaintances were a handful of co-workers from the airline I'd worked for and the people at my church. So, I asked myself how I could expand my circle to hundreds of people.

I started small with my own neighborhood and held a food drive there to meet my neighbors. Later, I hosted a Home Buyer's BBQ in my backyard. I partnered with a loan officer, made flyers and invited everyone, and I mean everyone, I knew to the BBQ.

Then I thought about all the places I did business as a customer--my hairdresser, my local coffee shop, mechanic, etc.--and I networked with the people who owned those establishments or worked there.

My advice is talk to everyone you know and if you don't know that many people, find ways to meet some. What do you like to do? Join a club, volunteer, join a service organization or the local chamber of commerce. Do things that genuinely interest you and that force you to meet new people regularly.

Get a coach. I've had a coach since I started at Keller Williams and meet with her weekly. A good business coach will help you remember the fundamentals and focus on your goals, which is especially important when you're starting out and everything feels new and overwhelming. Have them coach you on building a brand, on networking and communication skills. These things are important components of reaching your financial goals.

Develop an authentic and positive online presence. In many ways, being a real estate agent (or any business where you're front and center) is like running for political office. You must be clear and consistent in your messaging and you must be careful with your online image.

You are building your tribe of prospective clients with the things you post on your blog, website, Facebook page and Twitter account. Don't post anything you wrote after a stressful or frustrating day. Don't vent publicly about a bad experience with a client or colleague. Everything you write/tweet/post can influence a prospective client, so be thoughtful about the impression your online communications make.

Know your story. This is in the same family as knowing your value proposition and is also covered in the *IGNITE* class I mentioned earlier. But I think of this as the more personal version of your elevator pitch. Know why you're an agent; what it means to you personally to do this work; and the kind of experience you want your clients to have. Know it and be able to articulate it in 30-seconds or less.

Over the years my "why" has changed. In the beginning, I just wanted to have a flexible schedule, so I could be a good step-mom to my son. Each year, I set a goal and it's fueled by a different why. Your why might be to educate and influence people in the home buying process or maybe it's to raise money to support a charity. What's great about this is it's totally up to you!

Lead with revenue. Inspect what you're expecting out of the things you pay for. Meaning, I'm not going to invest in advertising or marketing without knowing how it will translate to more money in my pocket.

In the first year especially, you need money in the bank and there are loads of free and nearly free ways to network and market. My first year I spent almost nothing and today I don't spend any more than $50 on any one marketing activity. When you do start investing in marketing, think about partnering with someone else (loan officer, insurance agent) and split the cost, if it's more than a $50 investment.

Make your database(s) a top priority. You should have two parts to your database: your clients (past, present and prospective), and your vendor/business database. They are equally important and should be fed and updated regularly.

The first, the client database, is straightforward. Collect, at minimum, the names, addresses, phone numbers and email addresses for every client you have served, are currently serving, or may serve in the future.

The second, the vendor database, may be a new concept for you. This is a database of local small business owners to whom we can send business. Painters, plumbers, landscapers, architects and handymen are just a few examples. Our clients are always asking us for referrals and recommendations. By maintaining this database, we can be of continued service to our clients, and we are able to support small business owners. The added benefit is that as you cultivate these referral relationships, guess what? When those business owners hear that someone they know is looking for a real estate agent, you are top of mind.

We house our vendors in the "Favorites List" of the *HomeKeepr* app and provide free access to the list to all of our clients. I encourage you to download it and check it out.

HomeKeepr is a network of local Realtors and home professionals, such as plumbers, electricians, and painters who have been recommended, vetted, and hand-picked by other local home pros, Realtors and homeowners. *HomeKeepr* can help subscribers pick a professional when they need one, provide reminders when it's time for routine home maintenance tasks, and can store manuals and receipts for appliances, among other features.

You're a Business Now: How to Succeed at Self-Employment

One of the questions I get a lot when I speak with people who are interested in real estate careers is: what makes someone likely to succeed as a real estate agent?

It's a great question and an understandable one. Who wants to invest time, energy and money in becoming an agent if they're likely to hate it and/or fail?

What follows are some tips I'd share with anyone considering becoming a real estate agent at a brokerage where they'll have lots of autonomy. They probably apply to anyone considering self-employment of any kind though, so please read on even if a real estate career isn't in your future.

Stay humble. I have seen people make the mistake of believing that there is nothing they can learn from anyone else. This is totally untrue. I've been doing this since 2003 and I still look for opportunities to learn. I actively seek-out coaching from people who know more than I do.

Behave as if you're at work even if your office is in your home. Get dressed. Maintain a regular schedule. Avoid sending work emails while you're in the middle of doing yoga in your living room. Sometimes you do have to answer an email at 11:59 on a Thursday night, but to the extent you can, establish your working hours and stick to them. Plan days off and stick to those too.

Enjoy the freedom and flexibility, but not at the expense of the work. This is another common mistake I see agents make. If you don't wake up every day with the realization that, but for your own efforts, you are unemployed, you won't succeed. The freedom that comes from being able to set your own goals and design your own job is incredibly rewarding. But the people who are successful, balance that with accountability. They set clear goals for every day and are disciplined enough to meet them even though no one else is watching. You can probably train yourself to do this if it doesn't come naturally, but I find that a certain level of self-motivation and discipline is necessary.

Be yourself. This is such a cliché, but it's so important. You should know who you are as a real estate agent and be able to communicate that to prospective clients in a genuine way.

Have clearly defined goals and a definition of success. If you don't know where you're going, you won't know when you've arrived. Go through a formal goal-setting process regularly. How often really depends on your business. It can be something you do yearly, quarterly or monthly. But decide where you want your business to be at the end of that period.

Be a good boss to yourself. Pay yourself a salary, even if it's a small one when your business is just getting started. Have a plan for how you determine when it's appropriate to give yourself a raise. Invest in retirement; have a plan for taking a vacation or for when you're too sick to work; work the supplies you need into your monthly budget. In short, treat yourself the way you'd expect a good boss to treat you if you were their employee. Otherwise you'll resent yourself and burn-out.

The Part-Time Real Estate Agent

A quick disclaimer before we get started: It is possible to be a great real estate agent even if you aren't devoting 100% of your work life to it. (I started out part-time myself.) So, by no means do I want anyone to interpret this as a criticism of part-time agents. In fact, part of this chapter is about how to effectively serve your clients and make a living when real estate isn't getting 100% of your professional attention.

But it is also important for new agents to know some of the disadvantages to pursuing real estate as a side business or a part-time venture, and to have a plan for addressing those potential challenges.

Let's start with what I mean when I say "part-time." Unlike other jobs where part-time is defined by the number of hours you work per week, in real estate I think of part-time in terms of the professional attention and energy you're devoting to it. If real estate isn't your sole professional obligation--if it's not the only way you generate your income--then I consider you part-time for the purposes of this discussion.

There are many moving pieces when it comes to the laws, rules and forms that govern what we do and how we do it, and they are often changing. This is one of the challenges to being part-time. We have monthly trainings for agents at our office about all of that, *because* it's so important.

Attending trainings and getting lots of repetitions completing transactions, and their accompanying paperwork, is crucial to serving clients well and feeling confident as an agent. If you're working another full-time or part-time job, it can be difficult (and sometimes impossible) to attend those trainings, get that daily practice and stay on top of industry news and laws. And the consequences for missing something or making a mistake because there was a bit of information you didn't know, can be serious.

The more transactions you close, the better you get at negotiations. This is a critical point. The skill of negotiating and communicating on behalf of your clients is one you get better at the more you do it. It's like a muscle that gets stronger with training. I pay attention to things that the agents I'm negotiating with do and say. The things that are smart and effective, I remember and use myself the next time I'm in a similar situation. The things they do that are ineffective, I make note never to do. You can learn so much by observing agents on the other side of the table from you. Learn from their successes and mistakes.

You might be wondering what to do if being a part-time agent is the best fit for your life right now. As I said, I started out as a part-time agent, and I want to leave you with some advice if that's the road you decide to take.

There are two ways to structure a part-time real estate career that I think are solid approaches.

Join or build a team. On a team you could have someone to serve as your transaction coordinator. This person would manage the extensive paperwork process involved in the buying or selling of a property and provide you with accounting and administrative support.

Partnering with another agent is another option and it means that there's someone else who can hold open houses, show properties to clients, or conduct the initial meeting with prospective clients. You don't have to do it all, all the time. I have incredible resources about the most successful teams in the nation, so email me first and I can help connect you to the best of the best!

Build a career on referrals. Get your license but don't fully activate it. At Keller Williams, if you refer a client to another agent within the company you will receive a percentage of the commission on whatever transaction comes because of that referral. You don't show any homes, represent any buyers or negotiate any transactions in this career model. You get paid for making the connection between client and agent.

Where Do You Want to Be? Setting Your Sights on Your Goals

This chapter is all about deciding what you want and deciding how you're going to get there. Here's how I approach goal-setting.

Formal training through my brokerage. At Keller Williams we start big and then drill down to monthly, weekly and daily goals. I started with a course called, *Quantum Leap,* as a new agent and have taken it multiple times over the years. Gary Keller created this training course to help people set their five-year goals. The premise being that whatever big dream you have, you're five years away from achieving it. It takes that long to condition yourself, learn and hone new skills and make a plan--to build the foundation required to turn that dream into a reality.

The second formal goal-setting training I do is the *Business Planning Clinic*, in which I break my five-year goal(s) down to three-year goals and then from three-year goals to one-year. Once I have my goals broken down in this way, I use KW's CGI calculator, a mathematical calculation that breaks that one-year financial goal down to monthly, weekly, and daily activity goals. I literally come out of it with to-do lists for each day. (The mathematical calculation is based on your target income goal for the year.)

Accountability activities. Setting my goals is one thing, but I also need a formal accountability program to help me achieve them. If I never check in on my goals, I could get to the end of the year and be light years away from where I want to be financially. So, once per week my team reviews our goals vs. our actual numbers-- i.e. where we planned on being and where we actually are. Ideally those two things match!

I also meet with my KW coach weekly to review those numbers and set my goals for the following week.

Monthly, I participate in something called, *The 15th Protocol*. All the agents from our office meet on the 15th of the month to see whether we're on track for meeting our goals. The idea behind this is that if you aren't in good shape by the middle of the month and don't make any adjustments, you won't meet your goal by the end of the month.

And finally, I meet with the other agents in the top 20% (of transactions closed) in my office and we talk about our goals and any challenges we're facing.

This is one of the things that makes Keller Williams different. In a profession that many people assume is hyper-competitive, we have a team-oriented mentality. The profit-sharing model helps in this regard because we all sink or swim as a group. The other factor that contributes to this is the Associate Leadership Council. It's agents helping other agents. It's refreshing!

I'm clear about why I'm doing what I'm doing. The goals I've been talking about are financial goals--I decide how much salary I want to generate each year and I work toward that goal. But the motivation behind my goals changes from year-to-year. Beyond what I need to earn to support myself, I am often motivated by a mission or charity I want to support. For example, I can't go on a mission trip with my church (I've got family and work obligations that keep me here), but I can devote some of my salary to sponsoring people who can go and do that mission work. So, I might set a goal of giving $10,000 to sponsor three people on a mission trip and then I'm working toward my financial goals with that motivation behind it.

It's important to me to connect what I'm doing at work to whatever cause has spoken to me that year. I'm finding my "why," if you will.

What charities or experiences would be meaningful to you? Ask yourself how you could best support them or make them a reality through your work. Then you're starting to get closer to your "why."

Some of my goals are not financial. Sometimes my goals are relational. I might set goals related to how many new people I want to meet each week. Or sometimes it might be about serving a certain number of families. Other times my goals are related to the number of aspiring agents I can reach and coach. And sometimes I set goals for continuing education--trainings I want to attend or a specialized skill I want to learn that will help my business long-term.

I follow the SMART guidelines for goal-setting. In terms of the content of my goals, whether financial or action-oriented, I follow make sure they are: Specific, Measurable, Achievable, Realistic and Time-Bound.

The Value of a Coach

No one is going to knock on my door tomorrow if I don't show up to work and complete the tasks on my to-do list today.

That is one of the things I love about my career—I wake up every day and create my own job.

There is so much responsibility inherent in that, as well as a ton of freedom and joy in it. But being an entrepreneur can be a lonely place sometimes, and often we can't see ways we could be improving or pushing ourselves because we're too close to have any perspective or objectivity.

That is the beauty of a coach. They can help us with those things and much more. Here are just a few benefits of a coaching relationship.

They hold you accountable for meeting your goals. This is, arguably, the biggest advantage to having a coach. Share your SMART goals with your coach and agree that he or she will check-in with you regularly about your progress and challenge you when you don't meet them or when you don't do the things you promised you would.

You learn from someone who knows more than you or has a different area of expertise. You have access to information that you wouldn't have otherwise when you work with a coach. Knowledge it took that person decades to gain can be yours in minutes or hours.

You get honest feedback on your own performance. This is something that we have ready access to when we work for someone else in the typical boss-employee paradigm. But once you're working for yourself, or in an autonomous job (like real estate), opportunities for external feedback can be non-existent. As much dread as an annual performance review has conjured up for me in previous jobs, there can be great value in hearing where there is room for us to improve, grow or change professionally.

You have a sounding board and cheering section. Again, these are often lacking in the world of the entrepreneur. Even the most introverted among us needs to bounce ideas off other people from time to time. And even the most confident of entrepreneurs sometimes needs to hear some words of encouragement or a pep talk.

Just as a coach can see places where you can grow and improve, so can they see places where you are rocking this whole business-owner thing!

You expand your network. Networking is a word we hear repeatedly as entrepreneurs. I think it often gets conflated with "schmoozing" which we all have differing levels of comfort in doing. But really, networking is just about interacting with other people to exchange information and develop contacts. Building a relationship with a coach is a form of networking. They are learning about you and what you do. They might then refer other people they know to you for your services, or they might know people who can help you in some other area of your business.

You get inspired. Think about it. You saw the value in coaching and were assigned a coach. And then they *chose to coach you* because they saw something in you that was worth the investment of their time and energy. Wow! How do you not find the motivation to get up, get going on that project and succeed when someone like that believes in you?

Retiring Out of Real Estate

If you're scratching your head and wondering why in the world I'm talking about retirement in a book about getting started as a real estate agent, I don't blame you! But, stay with me.

Your retirement may be decades away. Even if that's the case, you should read on, because building your business so that you can one day transition out of it, is as important as building the kind of business you want to operate in the meantime.

My advice to you is to create a database of potential and existing clients, as well as people who refer clients to you regularly. Make sure that for everyone in your database you have, at minimum: their name, street address, email address and telephone number.

Feed your database continually with new people and with updates on existing contacts. Create something that will serve you well in your business, but that would be attractive and adoptable by another agent when you're ready to retire.

Which brings me to yet another way that retiring out of real estate might impact you. You might adopt a retiring agent's business.

From your perspective as the adopting agent, the financial benefits are obvious. However, you only want to pursue the adoption of another agent's business if you know you will have the time, energy and resources required to care for their clients as well as your own.

When the time comes to retire yourself, or to adopt another agent's business, you'll want to know which kind of retiring agent you (or they) are. Nick Krautter's book, *The Golden Handoff*, is full of important information and can help you make a plan for yourself and your business.

Whatever the level of involvement, you'll need to draft and sign a contract that clearly states the expectations and promises being made by both parties. You never want to simply purchase an agent's database for a lump sum. I am always looking to have conversations with agents about this and we are looking to partner with agents who want to sell their database base to our team. Reach out to me and let's talk!

Conclusion

Thank you so much for taking the time to read this book and to engage with the material. I trust it has helped you in at least a few concrete ways, and that it will serve as a resource for you in the future.

I've put together this booklet in hopes of making new friends and to grow my network so be sure to connect with me on FB.

I wish you all the best in your real estate career and hope you'll send me an email (rebeccad@kw.com) and let me know how you're doing!

Take care,
Rebecca

About Rebecca Del Pozo

In 2003, her first year at Keller Williams, Rebecca Del Pozo received the "Rising Star Rookie of the Year" award. Since then she continues to be recognized for her performance and to receive sales production awards from her brokerage.

Rebecca is proud to have served a large number of families in her career, which amounts to millions of dollars in real estate sold. She has ranked in the top 3% of the over 147,000 Keller Williams Associates worldwide for transactions closed.

Rebecca is the founder of Rebecca Del Pozo & Company, a team that consists of a Listing Specialist, Licensed Transaction Coordinator, Buyer Specialist, Showing Assistants, and an Administrative Assistant.

She has served on numerous committees and panels over the years, as well as in a leadership position within her own market center. In addition, Rebecca regularly teaches classes to other real estate agents and has been invited as a guest speaker to discuss hot topics in real estate many times over.

When she's not selling houses, Rebecca can be found pursuing her other passions: singing and sailing on her boat in the waters of the Puget Sound.

You can contact Rebecca at rebeccad@kw.com and friend her on Facebook!

Made in the USA
Middletown, DE
16 June 2021